The Weight of Worlds

Thomas Emmett Waggoner

This composition of thoughts

And collection of life and love

Is dedicated to my wife

What she has given me

And to the meaning of her name
…Kavitha.

Contents   *Page*

All Men are Holy

All men are holy
His thoughts inviolable
Whether of madness or genius
Fruition or intuition
His being profitable.
Only once will nature intersect
Bud and bring forth
Open, fold, and reopen.
And never again.
His spirit incorruptible
Borne of the same
Comprehension of the cosmos
That fuse us all.
His soul sacrosanct
His actions
Driven from imperishable thoughts
Over the universe of time and wonder
Intimate who he is
And from what shadows and depths
He has fortuitously emerged
Tirelessly upon the precipice of life.
His words
Ashes and sparks fired from
An inextinguishable hearth
Of vapors whose solid atmosphere is
Grasped from the medium around us
Dashed upon stone
Or cast as an orator upon the masses
Emanate not from the tenebrous underbelly
Of the unhallowed past
But of the bellows of the future
Making way for the present
And our fecundity
That in which his posterity will be sovereign.

TEW 12-25-05

All men are holy-Life Beyond Life

All men are holy
His thoughts inviolable
Whether of madness
Or genius
His being profitable.
Only once will nature intersect
Bud and bring forth
Open, fold, and reopen.
And never again.
His spirit incorruptible
Borne of the same
Comprehension of the cosmos
That fuse us all.

His soul sacrosanct
His actions infallible
His teachings timeless
For we are all crowned kings
In our domain
Our middle earth
For we are all men
All men have lived
And all men have died
But those who take death
Will be remember on our tongues
And in our hearts
In memories
Passed on and on.

Go, then…
Walk in the valley of
Light and Life
And mark the
Indelible ink of time
On your own story
Day beyond day
Life beyond life.

TEW 9/19/09

All Men are Holy-The Coming Year

We are all overgrown
With false hopes and decaying dreams
Tumult is upon us now
The world is too much for us
The fields are bare and in waste
Bereft of her fertility
And winter is soon coming
And when death comes thy way
Take him, do not let him take you
For we are all crowned kings
In our domain, our middle earth
For all men have lived
And all men have died
But those who take death
Are those remember in stories, on tongues, epithets
And in memoirs passed on and on…
Go, then and be those whom we reminisce upon
Be that which is always there.

TEW (date unknown)

All Men are Holy-The Dying Year

The dying year is no longer
To which this closing night is due
This heavy weight of hours
This rain and lightning has come and spread
As a sublunary vault
That will be awaken in the moments of the year
Of trumpets that drive our dead thoughts out of
Our minds and over the universe
That through these lips we are made holy again
As Spring has fallen
And winter comes
Will not Spring be far behind once more
And bud and bring forth again
Our inviolable man
Our sacred vision
The quiet susurrus before the storm
The impulse of our boyhood
The Season of Man remembered.

TEW 12-5-05

Brevity of Life

The Names we call Life and Love
The Names we call our world
This sublunary creation
This sylvan splendor
This blue island in the sea of cosmos
Globe of mankind
Rock beneath the firmament
Terminable realm under grace
Temporal home
Transient habitat
Prevaricator of the truth
Palace of irenic hopes
This earth.
This land before Elysium
This bivouac beneath the stars
It becomes and is the awakening of the senses
The quite susurrus before the storm
Little bits of steal pulled towards the magnet
Thoughts that dip the color palette
And paint the poet's tale
The kiss beyond the lake on the pebbles
The world we know
The times we live
The sustenance of our souls
Steal on the cutting board
Blood on the hand
Shame on the heart
Tears of the aggrieved
Lamentation for the lost
Departure of love
Bereaver seeking answers
Search for solace
Will of the redeemer
Grace of the sempiternal
Coming of the Creator
Brevity of life.
The brevity of this Life.

TEW 1/19/04

Concrete

Concrete are these walls
Beyond which are my thoughts
Concrete is my soul
In which I find rest
Concrete is the ground
From where I stand firm.

Firm is the theorem
From which I base
Life's calculations.
Concrete is the abstract
From where I create.

Create, I did, this concrete
From where I build life
Concrete is the fence
In which I stir my emotions
Bolden is the Love
Found deep in the Soul.

TEW 9/24/09

End

Beginning
Fallen
Arisen
Zero
Infinity
Life
Death
Inspiration
Expiration
Conception
Extinction
Birth
Grave
Fresh
Withered
New
Old
Young
Elderly
Black
White
Sunrise
Sunset
Rain
Clear
Zenith
Nadir
Peak
Trough
Celestial
Sublunary
Introspection
Extrospection
Evaporation
Sublimation
Trial
Tribulation
Friend
Foe
Start
Stop
Foreign
Domestic
Right

Wrong
Left
Right
North
South
Superior
Inferior
Medial
Lateral
Universe
Galaxy
People
Person
Lake
River
Gravity
Levitation
Axis
Atlas
Vertical
Horizontal
Latitude
Longitude
Water
Ground
Country
State
Tropics
Desert
Cold
Warm
Awake
Asleep
Dawn
Dusk
Alive
Dead
Heaven
Hell
Breathe
Apnea
Blood
Water
Smile
Frown
Erasable

Indelible
Empty
Full.

TEW 7/7/09

Esteem me not

Esteem me no longer as a night hawk
For the effulgent striking lights of dawn
At 6am come too soon
And with such an alacrity
That I can no longer seek refuge after twilight.

Looming in the airy night
Once captivated in gross chiaroscuro
Dancing in shadow
In the alertness of the sky
Intrepid, yet reckless
The ethos of his culture is void filling void

Mixed man, you are
Combined in the oil of the night
Wet canvas collecting content
And color
Groping soul
Toiling in a violable world
Seek the water, once again
The sacrosanct
The roborant milk and honey

Thus we travel in the morning hours
Thus we look and we see
Thus we walk a little further
And envelope those we know
And those we free

Esteem me not for the day is brighter
The night once thrilled and anticipating
Drains me now

Esteem me not
The hawk is dead

Esteem me now
The morning star has risen.

TEW 7/29/06

Finding Direction

You are at a pivotal time
When the fork in the road
Diverges
And you can take
The one less traveled by.
When you are David
And this sublunary world
Is Goliath.
When you are Ephesus
And Rome
Is a mighty bulwark.
You must always
Remember what life is
A collective idea
And spirit
Inspired by
The small things
In small moments
It is who we are when
The sun rises
And the sun sets
It is who we are
When we are lost among
The cosmos of creation
Or lost within the innermost
Sinews of the soul
There
And only there
Can you feel
The palpable fibers
Of truth
And what it is
That is absolute
In the soul.

TEW 1/25/08

Fishing for Truth (4/16/08)

Tarry not in the Sun of today
But in the Light of tomorrow.
Walk lightly in the burrows
Of bittersome society.
The veracity of the world
Will be known to man
When the world
Is removed from man.
The pangs of yesteryears
Sow the seeds of tomorrow.
You can handle the truth;
First you must seek it,
Although it is very close
To each of us.

The fish in your veins
Swims into strong waters of heredity,
At times it is washed back
By the head currents of the heart,
But it keeps leaping as the salmon
During spawning in the spring
And soon it sows the seeds
Of a new line
And casts off the road to perdition
That nearly took its life.

Swim on fish.
Into the head current
Fight the masses
And make headway for posterity.
Tarry not in the tepid pools of the stream,
But face front and stare down
The evolving waters of time
And leave the mark of truth
Wherever you pass.

The perpetual currents of life
Are like the masses of people
Pursuant of hedonistic liberties
And epicurean delight
And not the truth of man.

TEW (date unknown)

Fructuous future

I implore you to never stop
Continue daily
Go quietly
Sift softly

Be the ever discerning creature
That yields not before the weight of life
Plough your own furrow within this fructuous soil
Wherein rests liberty
Once wrested from the hand of tyranny

I implore you to never stop
Continue daily
Go quietly
Sift softly

Be the penetrating mind of singular vision
That wastes not time grappling between day and night
Nor whose eyes that become purblind by grandiosity
And lose sight of all glimmer and hope

Be that story of life, of truth, of tall tale
Of which our forefathers epitomize
The apotheosis of man loosing a struggle of life
Of that intersection of being
Vacillating between extant and extinct

But whose inane ethos breaks free
And takes flight to the heavens
Taking man in one fell swoop
From the base of his doom
To the crowning zenith of his victory

I implore you to never stop
Continue daily
Go quietly
Sift softly.

TEW 2002

Hunting Poem

Discovering your trail in the course of life.
To know that each man is sacrosanct,
is a creation; whether of madness or genius,
only once did nature insect and bear fruit in this sublunary world,
beneath the spread of the glowing lamp we call the sun.
To know that though we traverse time
and realm among the stalling winds of worlds apart,
we wait as intrepid soldiers hunting prey
in the stealth of the chilly fall morning
from a tree stand mounted against a firm yellow maple
bearing up its last color to the autumn frost
that blankets the carpet of the forest floor as we encroach upon time…
edacious time….incessantly fighting away demons of impatience
and the cold blusters of howling drafts
that shudder us up into the rugged edges of bark armoring the steady trunk
that is the life vein of the forest.
We wait.
We wait.
The depths of silence are shattered by the tiniest sounds of a twig snapping
in the darkness that is the last leg of the night
before early dawn streams life into a new day.
Our eye's shift to the point as if a current of electricity jolted through us.
Nothing.
Our vision is lost on the shadowing trees looming among the hillside…
protean shapes dancing in our mind.
Nothing.
Then at the last moment of time before calling it a day,
white shining twin peaks of ivory buck antler

Harness the first glinting rays of the sun as it sprinkles through the branches….
then and only then…
Do you ever feel that beast and man share the same destiny
as Mother Nature peels her way
through your veins.

TEW   2/14/2008

14

Ocean

If the ocean could save your soul
Or from the depths of the forest
There poured forth fresh life
Then man and beast would find respite
Beneath the nascent beauty of eternal light...
A light of friends, a light of foes,
A light of spring, a light of winter snows
A light of family and of face,
A light of truth and a light of grace...
So, I say to the many abroad...
Take your flag and raise it high, fly it brave,
Fly it nigh for all the liberties sought in vain
Be the intrepid soldier valiant in sand and rain
For in the end...children's lives will be saved
And matters such as this will be recorded to the grave
For all men die, but not all have lived...
To have lived and died
Is to have conquered the essence of creation...
For in the cradle of creation there lies the soul
That incorporeal spirit of eternal unrest
Of emotion, of life, of death and strife
So, count thy blessings, Foe and Friend
And ensure the fire still burns in the end
As the source of spirit, of ever-lasting being
As the soul of man, of woman and of believing.

TEW 4/26/04

Light The Night Each Day

Day is day
Night is dark
We are who
We are

Continue the time
Of seeing Forward

We just Can't seem
To get It right
Today

Continue the time
Of moving
Forward

Expect only what
You expect
Accomplish more than
You image

Dark is the night
But you can
Light the night
You can't darken
The Day

We can work
By Day
And by Lighting
The Night

So light
The Night
Each Day.

TEW 1-18-08

Lights and Shadows

Greying the light
That is Life

Shadows too soon
To be

Our lives begin
To die

Death takes
Our place

Forever lost
In this Life

Do not quietly go
Where life
Has no end

Rise to the light
Depths of Shadows
Below

This greying Night
Rage
Rage
Against
The Dying Light

Greying the light
That is Life

Shadows too soon
To be.

TEW 8/9/09

LOVE

I love you so clearly and satiably
So deeply and vehemently
So lustful and menacing
So sweet and fresh
So righteously and flawlessly

I love you like the known quiet
Susurrus
Before the storm
And the wrecked havoc
Lying once it has
Left

I love you like the dew drop
On a rose petal
That hangs effervescently
In the slow wakening
Of the day

I love you so passionately
So forthrightly
So exhaustively
So endlessly

That at this point
My mind is ignited
Simply pondering
Over you
As you caress
My thoughts
Fully unaware
Of your pull
On me
As you lie
Somewhere
Miles away.

What penchant
I have for you
What utterly ignorant
Blind fools love...
No...what truth
I have found
In you

What credence
And law
I have found
In you
What honor
And exemplitude
You have made
Me bud
Open fold crush
And reopen
In the cycle of life
That carries
The key
To the future.
What love I have found in you.

TEW 1/19/05

Mortui vivos docent

The deceased
Teach the living…
Is an idiom
Found etched
In the cold crevices
Of anatomy laboratories
Worldwide.

How true do these words ring
To all of life
To Medicine.
Profound as they may be
These words vastly understate
The purpose.

TEW 8/31/09

Mother Earth's Ultimate Malignancy

Perched on the precipice of life
The sea of lights
Blur in the icy haze
Inundate the slope
Beyond your feet

Stones crumbling
Loosely breakaway
Beneath the mounting pressure
Of your soft naked soles

Undulating in the forceful
Pockets of gusting air
Your weight falters
Swaying forward
In the chilled
Rhythm of the stroke

The bell strikes
The clock stops
Your time is suspended

Motionless.

As if all the tension
Between the worlds had been erased
And replaced by a single unifying foreboding
The past, a ghastly apparition
Gnawing at you
Pulling, straining, writhing
You down to the abyss
The future, a tempest untamed
Inveigling you for more

Tossed but not detached
You feel like a ship on the periphery of a storm
Skirting the torments
But not entirely untouched
By the Mephistophelian lapdog
Crouched at the base of your feet

Jolted suddenly.

From the flesh of your feet

Plunge new-fangled roots deep into
The red arid ground
Embedding in a foundation of life
Anticipating the night's treasures

Halted.

Though your mind remains imbued
In its inebriating effect
The fall was thwarted.
The souls of your feet
Have grown new hopes

Life will go on
The Road will continue
Your feet will touch new ground
You inhale the icy air
That now does not seem so piercing
As legions before
Failed to breathe

You are Spring and Autumn
And Spring again
The birth, death and rebirth of transition
Fresh buds burst up to the heavens
You open, fold, crush
And reopen
Breaching every barrier
You are given another name
And returned to the earth
To rest in her bosom

Clearings open inside you
As though some mystic threshold
Had been crossed-over
You become a believer.
And count the weightless seconds...
Wahad
Tintain
Thalatha…
You were suspended over
The sea of your unknown
Before Saving yourself from
Mother Earth's ultimate malignancy.

TEW 4/19/05

The World of Natural Possibility

The Oh, how unbeknownst to thee
Is the world of natural possibility
And the wonders whereby that might be wrought
The magic of nature the natives once sought
Mixed up in a place where no other thaumaturgy is used
These are the things in this life we must choose
To peddle papers along in the dim light
Or move westward into the favonian breeze this night.

Make thee honest
To thy self be charged
Know the prison is free
You are at large
Escape thee to where the world meets the end
Sail to the Orient and come around again
Thee, O Captain, master and commander of the sea
Charge thy men to circumnavigate thee
As the ocean is round
Back to Cape horn
And then to Cape Town.

No limit there is to the wonders at hand
Take to every beach just to feel the sand
From Hawaii, to Melbourne, to Bombay and the Mid-East
The world of natural possibility is certainly a moveable feast
No ends, all routes remain
Too many beds abroad where my head has lain
Pick a direction, have faith on thy side
Make the most of your dreams and possibilities wherein abide.

For all men are borne when nature intersects once
Budded and brought forth over the course of nine months
How many chances and courses have we seen since those days
The value of natural possibility is often clouded in haze
But there always remains man's most treasured ore
How little doth we know of kismet and what we live for.

TEW 1/1/03

One-Two

When you breathe
When you think
When you walk
When you drink

Your inner pump
Of life
Gives life
Every second
Every day
Every night
To the soul
To the tissues
To the organs
Of your corporeal
Being

The circulation
Of purpose
Of command
Of existence
Of Life

This cyclic One-Two
Is the coaptation of valves
Opening
And closing
In the very sinews
Of our preservation
Of Man

The Heart.

TEW 10/25/09

Our Attitude

Our attitude
Toward life
Determines life's attitude
Towards us.

From this
Stems
All
Direction

Our lives begin
To end

To end
The day we become
Complacent about things
That matter.

TEW
8/31/09

Search This Soul

Search me, Oh, God
And know this tenebrous heart
Try me, in this underbelly of life.
See into the caverns
Where spurts of light trickle
Through depths unknown
Huddled in the peripheries
Of this mind.

Send me beyond the grave.
Gather up what remains
Settled in the disquiet
Among the stones of my past
And the marble debased
Under the cold November rains.

Whisper once more
To this listening heart.
Burrow me out of the grottos
Where I have laid
Wounded in the soil
That has buried my ancestries
And my distant past.

Unearth me once more
From the sublunary loins
That have opened
And swallowed me whole.
Evacuate this body
From the sands of the dry season
And the murky mortar
That has moored my feet into the mud
Stopping me in the nebulous, sunless
Mouth of an animal I cannot enslave
On my own.

Lift this corporeal body
From the stagnant
Cesspool where it has plunged.
Rejuvenate this soul
Reforge this character
Open up the vein
Of rebirth
Breach every barrier

Calm the seas
Lift this corporeal body
From the stagnant
Cesspool where it has plunged
Within this bosom.

Open the clearings that you have
Granted entrance before.
Put me in the deep
Halcyon repose
Where I have comfortably
Laid as a child
As though some mystic threshold
Had been crossed-over
Let me become a believer again.

TEW 9/15/09

The Steady foot of Time

The Steady foot of Time
Carries us
From Youth to Age
Imperceptibly one day
At times, in a flurry
Of Rage
Insensibly we think
Time has no fight with us
We become unaware of burly beards
And shortened arms
Thinking to ourselves
Our prowess undiminished

Time passes
As we pass time unaware
Yet Men have not refrained
From marking the lapse of Time
In celebration.

Celebrating those whose lives
Have been devoted to the good
Of their kind, our kind
By signal days or months or years
Often by memorials of joy
And Achievement
Or of bitter and unforgotten sorrow.

And, as for the Nation or the race
Or the Man
So in his own life
Are there for each of us
Memorable days of sympathy in joy
And Sorrow.

Ever in the heart of this Man
Lies a nation of memorable days.

TEW 4/5/09

To My British Lit College Professora,

I wanted to thank you after class, but I'll do it now. I wanted to express my gratitude for your deep and sincere benignity for each of us as well as humanity as a whole. I have never, in my four years here at Denison, seen a professor willing expose his or her psyche and emotions as you have this semester. It not only permeated our innermost coverings, it imparted a greater sense of community within the class, and it instilled a true feeling that is as human as we all are, having sensitivity and love. I can say, without equivocation, that I am a better individual by having taken your class. It's been an honor. And, for things to change in this world, in these times we find ourselves, we must have instructors, professors, who are not afraid to reach out across barriers and share an emotional side of them insothat he or she can better touch an emotional side of the students. It's inspiring. I truly found a meaning in this class. Thanks.

TEW (senior year at Denison University, 2004)

The Dreamer's Dream

I dream, you dream, we all dream
The disparity amongst us lies in what we dream
Failing light, approaching night
Summon the ship up the stream
No longer in a silvery brook, or a fictional book
Cast about in quiet reveries
We are living in the time of the parentheses,
Not the dream, not what lovers seem
A great and yeasty time where uncertainty
Is a fiend.

Find yourself still in the deep misty wood
Rustling, chasing, you become the prey
Running, running, light has faded away
Falter, gasping, the beast near upon you
You start like you should
Over the cliff, praying, falling, falling
You stare into the abyss
And it stares back at you
No longer the dreamer.

The fear, half-truth being more pernicious than pain
Clutching the bed, you seek who's to blame
Watching, waiting, commiserating
Perspiring, crouching, lying
Prostrate you fall as the door is broken
There was no betrayal
Only your dream
Wishing to be opened.

TEW 11/18/04

The Play

The field is set
Enemies align

Captains step forward
Scouts emerge

The call
The cadence
The horn bellows

Down
Set
Blue-42

The ball is snapped
Worlds ignite

Helmets clash
Blows begin

The Battle is entrenched
Wings break free

The pigskin sails
Men break for the moment

Silent with focus
The rock crosses the goal-line

Touchdown!

TEW 10/2009

The Thin Line

When you have that Moment
In Life
Don't Ride that thin line
Between Life and Lost
Between flirting with winning
But so close to losing

Saddle up for the ride
But know the outcome
Before you embark
On thin ice

For drowning slowly
Is your only answer
To the melancholy of losing
What should be a winner

Know the thin line
In everything you do
For in the peripheries
Of our daily worlds
It could be Life and Death
The One With
Or the one with out.

TEW 10/25/2009

The Ride of Fear

The knowing
The thinking
Born into being
Thinking about doing
Doing becomes you
It becomes you
As you try to ride
Ride that thin line
Between Doing and chaos
Between life and lost
And grabbing that chaos
You wrestle it to the ground
Like a demon cobra
And when the fear
From the depths of bellows
Rises up from the belly
You use it
You conquer it
You use it
And conquer it
Because you know it's been there
For an eternity
For an eternity
Buried in a wasteland
And you take that skeleton chaos
In its every fiber and fear
You ride
You ride it to the gates
Of Hell
And send it back
You send it back
To the netherworld

You use it and conquer it
You chase it to the wasteland

You use it
You bury it
You breathe it
You ride that fear
Because fear is fear
And fear has no being.
Fear has nothing…
Except you to feed on.   TEW 3/21/09

The Weight of Worlds

What do I do with this beast
This demon
This tormentor
This prevaricator
Of my truth
The naked truth
Of my life
The weight that stands between me
And the world
And the world and the heavens

Have we all not known them
Had our own night upon night
Lying awake as they gnash at
Us from dark corners
And cold deceit
Whispering, taunting troublesomely

I inhale his fiery blast too often
Gulp down his irascible turbulence
Too frequently
Some perpetual maelstrom
Against my will
And choke in my sleep as he heaves
Calescent coals where I rest my head.

As if all the tension
All the steely flesh
And the crepuscular cloak
Between his world
And mine
Had been
Replaced by a single unifying foreboding
Gnawing at you
Pulling, straining, writhing
You down to the abyss
The past, a ghastly apparition
The future, a tempest untamed

Tossed but not detached
Your feel the iron weight
And realize the chain bound to your ankle
Clanks and coils its links
As you Skirt the torments

Of this world waiting for the next
Having been anchored to the
soil of your past and confined to the reach
Of man in the heavens
But not of God beyond the firmament

Though every man was borne
From the same threads of provenance
Of the same comprehension
In the cosmos
And every man dies
With his last breathe…
Every man suffers
In his own way.

I awaken my inner eyes
The fall was thwarted
My mind imbued in its
Inebriating effect
I am lost
I am found
In the midst
There I am

A tug raps my leg
The chain clangles down
And the temperate comes up
As the festooning putrid air
Of origins unknown in the earth
Open, fold, crush and reopen
Swallowing me
Into something more
Into substance with origins unknown
Depths and pain I dare not excite
But tirelessly arouse on their own
Before toiling the chain
Into its depths
And offering me up
Once again.

TEW (date unrecorded)

The Whispering

The whispering
It's the conscious
It's the life within
The swells of the soul
The sputtering and palpitations
Of our innermost being
Our self in its truest form
In its darkest chamber of any prison
Our heart.

The quiet susurrus
In the wind
The deathly smell of the lost
The fruit of all life
And the greatest mystery of life
Having faith in the unbeknownst.

Some things are meant to be know
Others excepted by faith
And others never meant to be made lucid
To the mind or the soul
For we live in a life that was not made
To be finished swiftly or easily or smoothly
The greatest mystery propounded to belief
Is that there is life
That through breathe
We can inhale the foundation
Of our being
Or all that we were meant to be
In this inner creation
In this globe of wonder
And world of ephemeral youth
And understanding
That we are the precise and exact result
Of the intersection of nature
That will only be as it is
And never again
That certain verities hold true
When life turns to the end
We all become equal
We all become the end of each other
We all die when our last breathe comes no more
For we are all only men.

TEW 7/5/07

Though much is taken

Though much is taken
Much Abides
Though we are made weak by Time and Fate
Much subsists
Though we are barren and bereft of strength
We are made strong in will
To strive and seek and not to yield.

Though darkness is behind us and a rift between
Much prevails
Though broad seas hasten towards our feet
Our boat does not tremble
Though our enemy lies in wait
We are undaunted.

Though our land is threatened by plague and pestilence
Much persists
Though the storm encroaches dark and threatening to our people
Many remain
Though earth becomes a fiery deception
We march on as intrepid soldiers and spirits of truth
Though we walk as shadows in the valley of death
We have no fear.

TEW 2000

To know

I want to know
What's around the
Bend

I want to know
What's down the
Street

I want to know
What's across the
Seas

I want to know
What's on the
Other side of the comets
The other side of the
Cosmos
What is in the
Inner consciousness of
Creatures.

I want to be the
Magellan of time
The Viking of tomorrow
The Vancouver
Of today…
To find the Northwest Passage
To see the rise of civilizations
And the fall of
Kings
The canonization of saints
And the Beheading
Of Queeens.

I want to know
The science of decay
From one world
To another

The part and particle
Of the sands of time.

TEW 9/13/09

To the Native

Bring your bow
And arrow
Bring your war paint
And horse

Move your people
To the mountains
There is no place
For peace pipes

War is upon you.

Who is to blame you
Your lands tilled dry
The water now toxic
Rivers bled to bone
Forests slashed and burned
Harvests left with the ghosts
Of Skeletons past

Plague follows the conqueror
Barren becomes the people
Wasteland engulfs the valley

Bedrock becomes the fertile ground
Creatures become extinct
As empires rise on the bones of
Others.

Take up your arms
Your bow and arrow
Your sword and shield
Your spear
Your flint and lock
Your rifle
Your cannon
Your submachine gun
Your humvee, tank, stealth,
And aircraft carrier
Your drone.
And fight only
The good flight.

TEW 10/25/09

War horse

I am still alive
Barely...
Breathing through
Only one nostril,
It seems at times
With the weight of
The past
Marching on my chest
Like a battle horse
Waiting to deflate me.

Where do I move
So that the great hooves
No longer pound my chest
If I move up
They crush my bowels
And if I go down
They bruise my head
My life blood has all but seeped
Out of my wound
And left me writhing
Weakly upon the dust
Of my bones.

I am still alive
Barely
Breathing through
Only one nostril
It seems at times
With the weight
Of tomorrow
Palpitating on my chest
Like the battle drums
Of civil war
Waiting to divide me
Against myself.

Where do I go
So that the one arm
Does not wrestle with other
If I go north
They reach below
For the other's vulnerable belly
If I go south

They pull up for
The tender flesh of the neck
Castigating the other…
Are they not equipoise
Are they not brothers
In consanguinity?

I am still alive
Barely
Breathing through
Only one nostril
It seems at times
With the weight
Of this day
Lying on my chest
Like a lapdog
Of the underworld
Panting hot feverish
Air upon my brow
Sending noxious
Choleric fumes
To the terminal ends
Of my lungs.

What do I do with this beast
This demon
This tormentor
This prevaricator
Have we all not had our own
Lying awake as they gnash out at
Us from dark corners…
I inhale his fiery blast too often
Gulp down his irascible turbulence
Against my will
And choke in my sleep as he heaves
Ignited coals where I rest my head.
No longer.

Never this one again.
I am not new to this old world.
It will have this bride no more.
This time I awaken my inner eyes
And focus the festooning putrid air
Into something more
Into substance with origins unknown
Depths and pain I dare not excite

Before blowing the flame
Right back down his throat.
He shall no longer have this chest to
Encroach upon.
No more will his wind
Engulf my seas
And swallow my conscious
No longer.

TEW 8/8/05

What Autumn Brings

The new season emerges
Loyal colors
Parading mascots
Raucous crowds

The Summer shies away
Like a salt block
In Water
The Past dimmed
Tides change
Spirits collide
Stadiums echo
The loyal stand tall
Hope is Reborn

We come together
To watch the
Titans clash
Teams compete
Players unite

The Game marches on
Rivals are re-lived
The gridiron smolders
As new champions
Are crowned

The new season
Emerges
The Game marches on
Under the dying
Light of summer.

TEW 9/4/09

Whisper Once More

Search me, Oh, Eternal
And know this tenebrous heart
Try me, in this underbelly of life
See into the caverns
Where spurts of light trickle
Through depths unknown
Huddled in the peripheries
Of this mind

Send me beyond the grave
From the violable to the sacrosanct
Gather up what remains
Settled in the disquiet
Among the stones of my past
And the marble debased ground
Under this cold November frost

Whisper once more
To this listening heart
Burrow me out of the grottos
Where I have laid
Wounded in the soil
That has buried my ancestors
And my distant precluded past

Unearth me once more
From the sublunary loins
That have opened
And swallowed me whole
Evacuate this body
From the sands of the dry season
And the murky mortar
That has moored my feet into the mud
Stopping me in the nebulous, sunless
Mouth of an animal I cannot enslave
On my own.

Lift this corporeal body
From the stagnant
Cesspool where it has plunged
Rejuvenate this soul
Re-forge this character
Open up the vein
Of rebirth

And let the sanguinity
Of life ebb and flow
Breach every barrier
Calm the seas
Lift this corporeal body
From the stagnant
Basin where it has plunged
Within this bosom

Open the clearings that you have
Granted entrance before
Put me in the deep
Halcyon repose
Where I have comfortably
Laid as a child
As though some mystic threshold
Had been crossed-over
Let me become a believer
Again.

TEW fall 2005 (revised 12/10/05)

Wreckless abandon

In space
In time
We wonder

We wonder of the perceptions of individuals
In a huddle of inequality among races
The manifestation of good
Within an evil swells
And pours forth from the cracks of evil
God-like drips
As a dewdrop from the petal
Of a human soul
A rose.

TEW   11/18/09

You

You are
Whatever you
Are

You are
What you say
You are

You are
What you think
You are

You are
Everything you
Make yourself
Out to be

But you are
Only *who* you are
When you are
Alone.

To be Alone
And still be
Who you truly Are…
This is You.

TEW 10/25/09

Zarzuela

Perhaps it was the romantic tales
Perhaps the harmonious blend
The undertones of spice and fruit
Richness as deep as love
Fulfillment as pleasurable
As youth.
It's as red as earth
Fresh as plums
As balanced as
The seasons.
Red wine.

TEW 9/2009

Passion

Burning, yearning
Still believing
Trying, lying
Still deceiving

Lust and love
Like water and oil
Mixing, matching
But always relapsing

Sleeping, curling
Still caressing
Seeping, Weeping
Still competing

Fleeting….passion
Exuding…passion.

TEW 2/2/10

Incipit Vita Nova

I'm fallen…
Fallen
Fallen

The waves are…
Fallen
Fallen
Fallen

These are the
Times…The
Times

That try men's souls.

We live and die
We laugh and cry
What we have is…you
What we have is…true

The new life…
Begins
The new life…
With glim---ers
Of Hope

TEW 2/2/10

Cheers!

Here's to Us
Here's to You…

Here's to All the Friends
That We once knew

Here's to the future…
And what it may Give

Here's to our friendship
That it may always Live

Here's to laughs
Here's to tears

Here's to cries…
And here's to Cheers
Cheers!

TEW 11/2002

Americano Fever

This land of lands
The dream of dreams
Emotions living
We are...we are
The driver of the driven
We live alive
We live palpably
We live raw

To think we once
Were jailed
Broken behind bars
Bailed...
Only by dreams
The feverish rally
Of Patriotism
Of Freedom

We've come down
Through the ring of fire
We've come down
Through the cracks in earth
We've come down
Through the storms of seas
We go on because
The fever is contagious...
And you only have
The courage of your
Convictions.

TEW 1/23/10

All Men Are Holy-Amen

All Men are holy
To know every man
Is a remarkable phenomenon
His story profitable
His being unique
To know that only once
Will nature intersect,
Bud and bring forth this person
And never again
Is sacrosanct
His flesh and blood sacred
His life representing a road
His dreams
Whether of madness or genius
Fulfilling the will of nature and kismet.
What makes his story different
Is the richness and profundity
Of each man's experience
And his understanding of himself
With one another
With each of us.

For all men die
But not all have lived.
To have lived and died
Is to have conquered
The essence of creation
To have walked as shadows
In the valley of Death
To have riddled the tombstone
Of destiny
And laughed
In the face of Fate
To have cried at the hands
Of family
And rejoiced in the hearts
Of friends.
To have loved
And been loved.
This is to have lived
And this is to have died.
And when Death comes thy way
Embrace him
And rejoice

As the world cries
As you cried and they rejoiced
When you entered the world.
Go, walk then in the light.
Seek and you shall be found
In a new life
In the firmament above the clouds.
Laiden and blessed in white
There you shall live again.
Amen.

TEW 9/10/05